THE
CONTINUAL
CONDITION

also by **charles bukowski**

available from Ecco

The Days Run Away Like Wild Horses Over the Hills *(1969)*

Post Office *(1971)*

Mockingbird Wish Me Luck *(1972)*

South of No North *(1973)*

Burning in Water, Drowning in Flame: Selected Poems, 1955–1973 *(1974)*

Factotum *(1975)*

Love Is a Dog from Hell: Poems, 1974–1977 *(1977)*

Women *(1978)*

play the piano drunk like a percussion instrument until the fingers begin to
bleed a bit *(1979)*

Shakespeare Never Did This *(1979)*

Dangling in the Tournefortia *(1981)*

Ham on Rye *(1982)*

Hot Water Music *(1983)*

War All the Time: Poems, 1981–1984 *(1984)*

You Get So Alone at Times That It Just Makes Sense *(1986)*

The Movie: "Barfly" *(1987)*

The Roominghouse Madrigals: Early Selected Poems, 1946–1966 *(1988)*

Hollywood *(1989)*

Septuagenarian Stew: Stories & Poems *(1990)*

The Last Night of the Earth Poems *(1992)*

Screams from the Balcony: Selected Letters, 1960–1970 *(1993)*

Pulp *(1994)*

Living on Luck: Selected Letters, 1960s–1970s (Volume 2) *(1995)*

Betting on the Muse: Poems & Stories *(1996)*

Bone Palace Ballet: New Poems *(1997)*

The Captain Is Out to Lunch and the Sailors Have Taken Over the Ship *(1998)*

Reach for the Sun: Selected Letters, 1978–1994 (Volume 3) *(1999)*

What Matters Most Is How Well You Walk Through the Fire: New Poems *(1999)*

Open All Night: New Poems *(2000)*

The Night Torn Mad with Footsteps: New Poems *(2001)*

Beerspit Night and Cursing: The Correspondence of Charles Bukowski and
    Sheri Martinelli, 1960–1967 *(2001)*

sifting through the madness for the word, the line, the way: new poems *(2003)*

The Flash of Lightning Behind the Mountain *(2004)*

Slouching Toward Nirvana *(2005)*

Come On In! *(2006)*

The People Look Like Flowers at Last *(2007)*

The Pleasures of the Damned: Poems, 1951–1993 *(2007)*

THE CONTINUAL CONDITION

{ poems }

CHARLES BUKOWSKI

edited by john martin

An Imprint of HarperCollinsPublishers

Originally published as a hardcover edition in 2009 by Ecco, an imprint of HarperCollins Publishers.

FIRST ECCO PAPERBACK EDITION PUBLISHED 2010

Designed by Mary Austin Speaker

Library of Congress Cataloging-in-Publication Data is available upon request.

ISBN: 978-0-06-177121-7

23 24 25 26 27 LBC 20 19 18 17 16

acknowledgments

Thanks to Bottle of Smoke Press and X-Ray Book Co.,
who first published several of these poems as broadsides.

contents

died 9 april 1553   1

thanks for the luck   3

my art form   4

rejected   5

full circle   8

the continual condition   9

let's have some fun   10

to kiss her long dark hair   11

waste   13

the recess bells of school   15

the wasted profession   17

the strange morning   18

feeling good in the new neighborhood   24

this kind of fire   25

unemployed   26

tough cob   28

the last race   29

my soul is gone   31

the theory   33

more than ow   35

dog times   36

I might get traded   37

faux pas   **38**

about a worried reader of my works: **40**

the agnostic   **42**

a good place   **44**

the legend   **45**

you've seen it on the barstool next to you—   **47**

never   **48**

a hot sweaty day in August   **50**

news item   **53**

comeback   **54**

this flag not fondly waving   **55**

mannequins   **62**

my answer   **64**

under the suckerfish sun   **65**

I am chastised   **66**

a fine madness   **67**

a consistent sort   **69**

the old movie star   **70**

trying to dry out   **73**

consummation   **76**

before the 7th race   **77**

morning after   **78**

heavy dogs in cement shoes   **81**

down the hatch   **91**

tragedy?   **93**

listening to the radio at 1:35 a.m.   **94**

perfect silence   **95**

mirror mirror on the wall   **97**

parts dept.   **98**

dear editor: **99**

lack of a common interest   **101**

I'm upstairs now   **103**

as Buddha smiles   **104**

what have I seen?   **110**

a correspondent wrote bitterly: **111**

moving toward age 73:   **112**

I saw a tramp last night   **113**

mountain of horror   **114**

the last winter   **124**

bent   **125**

bayonets in candlelight   **126**

THE
CONTINUAL
CONDITION

died 9 april 1553

in bed with the flu and reading Rabelais
as the cat snores
the bathroom toilet
hisses
and my eyes burn.

I put Rabelais down
and blink.
this is what
writers do
to each other.

for him, I
substitute
a tab of
vitamin C.

if we could only swallow
death
like that (I think we
can)
or that death would
swallow us
like that (I think it
does).

life is not what
we think it
is, it's only what we
imagine it to
be

and for us
what we imagine
becomes
mostly so.

I imagine myself
rid of this
flu.

I see myself parading the
sidewalks again amongst the
sharks
of this world . . .

meanwhile, the cat, like most other
things, pushes too
close;
I move him
gently away, thinking, Rabelais
you were a
mighty mighty interesting
fellow.

then I stretch out as the ceiling
watches me and
waits.

thanks for the luck

at this time
I no longer have to work
the nightclubs, the universities,
the bookstores
I no longer have to tell the freshman English class
at the U. of Nebraska (Omaha)
at 11 a.m. while sitting
at a yellow elevated desk
why I did it
how I did it
and what they might do in order to do
it for
themselves.

I don't mind the plane flights back
with the businessmen
all of us drinking doubles
and looking out past the wing
trying to relax
grateful that we were not on skid row
knowing we had certain abilities
(so far)
which have saved us from that.

I may have to do it all again, but
right now I am where I belong:
passing over my own Grand Canyon
on schedule
no seat belt
no stewardess
no lost luggage.

my art form

I watch the jocks come out in the
post parade. one will win the race. the others will
lose. but each jock must win sometime in some race
on some day, and he must do it often enough. or he is
done as a jockey.
it's like the girls on the street trying to score for
their pimp
or each of us sitting over a typewriter tonight or tomorrow
or next week or next month
and doing it well enough
once in a while
or he is done as a writer,
he's a whore who can't score.

I think I would like a little more kindness
in the structure
but the nature of things has a way of not
listening.

when I was a boy I used to dream of becoming
the village idiot.
I used to lie in bed and imagine myself the
happy idiot
able to get food easily
and easy sympathy,
a planned confusion of not too much love
or effort.

some would claim that I have succeeded.

rejected

it was when I was living down on DeLongpre
and writing dirty stories for the sex mags
I never got a reject
until one day I got one
an irritating one:
"dear Chinaski:
this is well-written but
to infer that an ugly man your age
had sex with four women in one day
is simply infantile
day-dreaming."

I stood there looking out the window
at the sunny day, the sidewalk, the
lawn.
"come here and give me a little kiss,"
said the lady on the couch.
the phone rang.
"hello," I answered.
"listen, you bastard, I know you've got
somebody there now! I'm psychic!"
she hung up.
"do you like me in this dress?" asked
the lady on the couch.
the phone rang again.
"hello," I answered.
it was another lady:
"I want you to come over tonight."
"who is this?" I asked.
"this is Vera," she said.
"I'll be there," I answered and hung
up.

"do you think I've put on too much
weight?" asked the lady on the couch.
"listen, Susie, we've already had sex,
I need some rest," I told her.
she picked up her purse, opened the door,
slammed it and was gone.
I threw the story and rejection into the
wastebasket.
a red car drove up on the lawn.
a lady got out.
she knocked on my door and I opened it.
"listen, you son-of-a-bitch," she said,
"I saw that woman leaving! who was that
woman?"
"just a friend, nobody important," I told
her.
"well, she god-damned better not be!" she
said.
"she's too fat," I said.
"come on," she said, "let's go into the
bedroom and lie down a while."
I followed her in as the phone rang.
"aren't you going to answer it?" she
asked.
"no," I said, "it's nothing."
I sat on the edge of the bed and started taking
off my shoes.
she stood there unfastening things.
"how's the writing coming?" she asked.
"it gets rough sometimes," I told her.
"how come?" she asked.

"the god-damned editors don't know anything,"
I answered.
"what do you mean?" she asked.
"I mean," I told her, "that I get rejected for
the wrong reasons."
she slid under the sheets as I sat there
naked.
"do you ever get rejected for the right
reasons?" she asked.
"hardly ever," I answered, sliding under the
sheets.
"do you like me?" she asked.
"I wish," I told her, "you wouldn't wear all
that mascara, it makes you look like a god-
damned whore."
"don't you like whores?" she asked.
then her head was under the sheet and I
couldn't see her anymore
but I could make out
this round object sliding
toward my center.
"now wait," I told her, "you don't have to do
that if you really don't want to . . ."

full circle

Sanford liked to play dirty
tricks like piss in milk bottles,
burn the legs off of spiders, torture
dogs, put water in gas tanks, etc.

he was full of dirty
tricks.

we grew up together.

when World War II arrived he enlisted in the
Army Air Force.

"the flyboys get all the pussy," he
told me.

on his second mission over the English
Channel they
blasted his ass out of the
sky.

they never found him.

another dirty trick in a dirty trick
world.

the continual condition

all up and down the avenues
the people are in pain;
they sleep in pain, they awaken
in pain;
even the buildings are in pain,
the bridges,
the flowers are in pain
and there is nothing
going to
release it,
release us;
pain sits, pain floats, pain
waits;
pain is.

the music is bad
and the love
and the script

in this place now
as I type this

or as you read this
in your place now.

let's have some fun

there will always be people who say, let's go on a boat or
let's go to Argentina or let's go to a movie or let's go to a
tennis match or let's visit my sister
or how about a picnic?
and
I don't understand any of this
because to me
just walking across the room is like walking through flames
and
the first strange face I see each day
adds a knot to my stomach
and
I don't have the time because
I haven't paid the gas bill
or checked the air in my tires
and
one of my teeth is aching (*on the left side*)
and I've received several letters in the mail from crazies
and there's a notice from the government about a tax matter
and I need an oil change (*and my car needs one too*).

there's a fellow down the street and he just sits on his porch.
there are people who just sit a lifetime with unblinking eyes.

these could be the wise ones.
I am not one of the wise ones.
I even fight dragons in the dungeons of my sleep.

so if you want to send me to an early hell
then force me to spend an entire day at Disneyland.

to kiss her long dark hair

sweating in the kitchen
trying to hit one out of here
54 years old
fear bounding up my arms
toenails much too long
growth on the side of one leg.

the difference in the factories was that
we all felt our pain
together.

the other night I went to see the
great soprano
she was still beautiful
still sexy
still in personal mourning
but she missed note after note.
drunk,
she murdered art.

sweating in the kitchen
I don't want to murder art.

I should see the doctor and get that thing
cut off my leg
but I am a coward
I might scream and frighten a child
in the waiting room.

I would like to comfort the great soprano
I'd like to kiss her long dark hair.

and then there's Lorca still down in the road
eating Spanish bullets in the dust;
and the great soprano has never read my poems
but we both know how to murder art
how to drink and mourn;
sweating now in this kitchen
the formulas are gone
the best poet I ever knew is dead
and abandoned in the dust;
the others write me letters.

I tell them that I want to comfort
both Lorca and
the great soprano
but they write back about other
things
useless things
dull things
vain things.

I watch a fly crawl on top of my radio.

he knows what the answer is
but he can't talk to me.

waste

"boring," he said from his deathbed,
"I bored everybody, even
myself.
I wasted it, I was a fake, a word-
blower . . . all too fancy . . . all too
full of tricks."

"oh Master," said the young poet,
"that's not true at all, not at
all."

"all too true," said the old man.
"my work was overblown
rubbish."

the young poet did not believe
those words.
he could not, he would not,
for he too was writing
rubbish.

but still he asked the old man,
"but Master, what is to be
done?"

"begin at the beginning."
said the old man.

a few days after that
he died.

he had not wanted to see the
young poet anyhow.

now that didn't matter
either.

the recess bells of school

my father's feet stank and his smile was like a
pile of dog shit.
whenever I noticed the brisk hard stubble hairs of his
beard left in the bathroom basin
sickening thoughts would enter my skull,
I'd sense arcades fat with fools forever.

to be the very blood of that hated blood
made the windows intolerable,
and the music and the flowers and the trees
ugly.
but one lives: suicide before the age of ten
is rare.

brutal were the calla lillies
brutal the nectar and the kiss
brutal the recess bells of school.
brutal the softball games
brutal soccer and volleyball.
the skies were white and high,
and I'd look at the faces of the game-
players
and they were strangely masked.

now I eat in cafes
attend concerts
live with women
gamble
drink
trim hedges
buy automobiles
have friends and

pets;
I attend weddings
funerals
boxing matches,
I pay a fair share of taxes,
I stand in line at supermarkets,
I clean my fingernails,
I cut the long hair out of my nostrils,
I take sunbaths,
I repair damage,
I attempt not to offend,
I laugh,
I listen to the viewpoint of enemies,
I telephone plumbers and lawyers,
I get towed in from freeway breakdowns,
I get my teeth cleaned,
I search for heroes,
I go blind when I look too long at the sun.

my father's feet stank and his smile was like a
pile of dog shit.

everywhere
it's all the same.

the wasted profession

all the words, you know, it's hard to tell if you're truly on course or
on some vanity trip: how much can be said, how much has
already been said, and why?
other writers' words do me little good, then, why should mine be
special?
all my words . . . do they create
laughter through the flame?

the same poets reading over and
over again in the same venues; I am embarrassed for them and for
myself:
do we really think that we are fashioning speech more un-
usual than a stock market or weather
report?

all the words—we type away—on and on—most of us living lives
ordinary and without courage—are we sick to think that our
speech is
exceptional?

I don't like us and I never did—is there anything worse
than a creature who lives only to write
poetry?

the strange morning

it had never happened before and one doesn't
know why such things
happen.

it was about 11 a.m. and I had stepped
outside the bar for some air.
Danny walked up and I started talking
to Danny.
then Harry walked up and joined us.

then two other men started talking
to each other a few feet away.

"let's go back for a drink," I said to
Danny and Harry.

"no, it's nice out here," said Danny,
"let's gab a while."

so we did.

then I noticed some other men
standing about.
some were talking, others were
just standing there.

it all happened slowly.

more and more men arrived
and stood
at the corner.

it was getting crowded.
and it was getting
humorous.

there was something
strange in the air,
you could feel it.

there were many voices
now.
and more men arrived.
I don't know where they
all came from.

they stood around
talking,
laughing,
and smoking
cigarettes.

Jim the bartender stuck
his head out the door
and asked,
"hey, what the hell's
going on out here?"

somebody laughed.

Jim went back inside to
the empty bar.

it began to feel very
odd

as if the world had
decided to be transformed,
all at once.

there was a feeling of
joy and gamble in
the air.

I believe that everybody
felt it.

a great energy was
let loose and working
on everything.

then Jack the cop
walked up.
"hey, you guys,
break it up!
what the hell is going
on?"

we all knew Jack,
we drank with him
at night.

soon Jack was standing there,
talking and listening
to the others.

Danny grinned, "Jesus,
this is very strange."

"I like it," I said.

the whole corner was
crowded with
humanity
finally cut loose and
free,
laughing.

cars stopped and the
drivers looked out
wondering what was
happening.
we didn't
know.

finally I said,
"I can't stand this
anymore, I'm going in
for a drink."

Danny and Harry
followed me
in.

soon a few others
followed.

"lot of guys out there,"
said the bartender.

"yeah," said Harry,

"where are the
women?"

"the women don't
want anything to do
with bums
like us,"
said Danny.

we each had a couple
of drinks.
it took maybe 15 or
20 minutes.

then I went to the
door and looked
out.
everybody was
gone.

I came back and
sat down.

"wonder where they
went?"

"strangest morning of
my life," said
Danny.

"yeah," said
Harry.

we sat there thinking
about it.
then Danny started
talking about how his
family was going to
throw him out for
not getting
a job, etc.

Jim the bartender
stood there polishing
glasses
and things were back
to normal,
even to wondering
who was going to
buy the next
round.

feeling good in the new neighborhood

my neighbor, his name is Charley.
he caught me trimming my hedge
and he tells me
his business is doing a million
dollars a year,
and I tell him,
"that's great, Charley."

he runs up the red, white and
blue on his flagpole every
day, takes it down at night,
you can't blame him.

he's 83 years old and has a fat dog
named Hildegard.

in the old neighborhood
I used to be afraid to go into my
kitchen during bad moments
because
the butcher knife was in there.

now I sleep with a switchblade
under my pillow,
more for them than for
me.

this kind of fire

sometimes I think the gods
deliberately keep pushing me
into the fire
just to hear me
yelp
a few good
lines.

they just aren't going to
let me retire
silk scarf about neck
giving lectures at
Yale.

the gods need me to
entertain them.

they must be terribly
bored with all
the others

and I am too.

and now my cigarette lighter
has gone dry.
I sit here
hopelessly
flicking it.

this kind of fire
they can't give
me.

unemployed

fight we would
and I'd tell her
we're out of drinks now
I'm broke
you've got your cunt
you can go out and hustle more drinks while
I sit here looking at these god-damned walls.

you mean there's no more to drink?

no
but shit
you love me,
remember?

I hate you.

she would leave
she would grab her purse and be gone.

I'd go around sipping.
I'd sip almost-empty bottles and cans.
I'd look under the bed and couch for more.

at times like that you get to know a hotel room well.
you look at the venetian blinds and the hot plate.
you look at a newspaper on the rug.
the page looks at you and reads the same way over and over.

but when she comes back
it begins all over again

she asks
why are you so mean?

dear reader,
do you know something?
those who keep asking the same question
really don't want to hear the answer.

tough cob

we tend to like those artists
who starved or went mad or killed themselves
and were discovered afterwards.
it happens often
because great talent is usually fifty to
one hundred years ahead of its
time.

most of those acclaimed in their
lifetime
are mediocre performers.
of course, this is common knowledge,
so common that many of those who are not
recognized in their time
believe that this is a sign of their own true
genius
and countless wives, children, relatives,
friends and bystanders
must suffer
because of this illusion.

to laugh truly is to continue anyhow.

the last race

a fat Mexican woman in line in front of me
lays down her last two dollars, all in change,
quarters, dimes and nickels
as she calls the wrong number
and I walk up, bet twenty win and call the
wrong number as
a fart of thunder erupts from the sky followed
by a distant flash of light
small drops of rain begin their work and we
go out and watch the last race:
12 three-year-olds at a flat mile, non-winners
of two races
they break in a spill of color and chance
fight for position on the quick turn
enter the backstretch before the enchanting
mountains
there's still a chance for everybody
except then the six horse snaps a front
foreleg and
tosses a millionaire called Pincay to the
hard ground as
some of the poor groan for him
others don't care
and a few are secretly delighted
as the track ambulance circles counter-
clockwise
the race unfolds unfolds
as three contenders straighten out for the
stretch drive;
the favorite gives way
falls back
as the second favorite and a twenty-six-to-one shot

drive to the wire as one 8-legged creature
the last head-bob in the photo belonging to
the long shot.
as most of us tear up our tickets and begin our
walk to the parking lot and to whatever is
left for us
the drops of rain increase
become cold
and all we hope for is that our automobiles
will still be there
as Pincay regains consciousness in the track
infirmary and asks, "what the hell
happened?"

my soul is gone

the phone rings.
I have just finished a grapefruit.
it is the editor of one of the leading
sex mags of the nation.
"Charles Bukowski?" he asks.
"yeh?"
"listen, we want you to write us a
short story. we haven't heard from you
in a long time. what you been doing?"
I bite into a piece of toast, well-buttered,
then let him hear it around the
mastication:
"screenplay, horses, drinking. yeh."
he answers: "well, send us something soon,
will you?"
I say, "yeh." let the phone fall back into the
cradle.
now I've got to dream up some realistic
murder rape fantasy to
make the people happy.
it doesn't please me.
I open a couple of cans of cat food and
feed the cats.
one will only eat tuna
the other just beef-and-hearts.
they both bend over their dishes and show me
their dry and ridiculous bungholes.
well, shit,
will I go to the racetrack or will I rip off
a quick sex story for one grand?

on the freeway I open the sunroof and
my writer's locks blow in the California
75 m.p.h. wind.

I can do the story tonight.
meanwhile
I can check the whores at the racetrack
bar.
they are all wearing slit dresses now,
slit right up to the hip.
some wear panties.
the best
don't.

I get to valet parking.
the attendants all know me.
one of them hands me my parking tab,
asks, "how ya doin', champ?"
I grunt, give him a nod, climb out,
stretch,
jerk my right shoulder,
and move slowly off toward the
clubhouse.

the theory

I never had a problem getting
a job, though I had no trade.
a friend of mine told me it was
because I was so ugly, they knew
that if they hired me that I would simply
be glad to have any job and that
I would stay.
this could have been true but my
friend Bob was wrong on the second
point: I seldom stayed long:
oftentimes one week, sometimes two
or three, or a month at most.

my friend was considered intelligent
and talented
and he explained to me that night
while we were working overtime
that many people were afraid to
hire intelligent men such as he
because they knew men such as he
would surely move on.

he told me that 12 years ago.

and now when I meet somebody
on the outside from the factory
and I ask them,
"by the way, is Bobby still there?"

the answer is always the same:
"oh yes, he's still there . . ."

well, one thing they've got there
for the employees is this great
parking lot, 3 levels, but the cafeteria
is lousy
and the work is dreary and debili-
tating,
but my friend Bobby, he'll always have
a nice place to
park
his
car.

more than ow

finished in the aftermath,
pummeled in the shade,
left to rot on the bank,
tousled,
doused,
struck through,
oh, mama, sing songs to
me!
I can't handle this
action.
I need more light, more
light, more light
now!
the pig is under the
blade,
the soprano screeches
inanities,
the dice come up
snake-eyes.
I can't hold much
longer as
the troops from hell march
through
me.

dog times

in that hotel in Germany
that fancy hotel
across the park from the giant
water tower
I drank quarts of wine
locked myself in the bathroom
both late at night
and early in the morning
bellowing sad songs of
3 decades past.

Linda begged me to stop
and the phone kept ringing
but the police never
came
although I'm sure I kept
many people
awake.

for that
I'm sorry.

I bellowed those sad songs
of
3 decades past
locked in the bathroom
because I knew I didn't
belong anywhere
especially
being accepted as a
great American
writer.

I might get traded

they sent the veteran second baseman
down to Fresno
so a 22-year-old kid could have
his playing time.

it's a matter of investment:
cheaper help
with a future.

life in baseball
is limited.

but with a little luck in the Arts
you might last
right up to your deathbed.

unfortunately
it took me
half an evening
just to write this.

it looks like
another slow night in
San Pedro.

faux pas

at the track today
they were putting them into
the gate
and I hadn't gotten my bet down
yet.
the fellow ahead of me
seemed terribly slow in
making his
transaction.
he was fumbling
awkwardly
so I hollered at
him:
"COME ON! COME ON! PICK
UP YOUR FUCKING
TICKETS!"

the people in the
other lines
looked at
us.

"COME ON! PICK 'EM UP,
BUDDY!"

then the fellow
turned.
he had
no
hands.

yes,
I got my bet
down.

and
my horse ran
last.

about a worried reader of my works:

but what will you write about?
he asks.
you no longer live with
whores,
you no longer engage in
barroom brawls,
what will you write
about?

he seems genuinely concerned
that trouble will not
find me
or that I will not seek it
out.

I tell him that
trouble always arrives,
not to worry about
that.

but he doesn't want to
believe
me.

he seems to think that
I have manufactured my
life
to suit my typewriter
and if my life gets
good

my writing will get
bad.

but what will your public
think? he asks
about your living in a nice
house and having money
in the
bank?

they can still read Norman
Mailer, I tell
him.

but you're different than Mailer,
he says.

not at all, I say,
we're both about 25 pounds
overweight.

wondering,
he stares at me through
gray beard
eyes.

the agnostic

I've come off a week of the flu
just in time
to face the oncoming Christmas
season,
and do you realize the hopeless
crazy feeling this brings to an
agnostic?
it's as if the whole world has gone
sick on cue
people swarm everywhere,
everywhere,
everything's cluttered, jammed,
overloaded, jarring, inefficient
and stupid beyond
belief.
almost everybody is overwhelmed.
I myself have purchased a huge green
dead tree
and there it sits in my front
room.
any complaint I might make against
Christmas is nullified by this very
action.
I am screwed.
I have screwed myself again.
I resent screwing myself.
I resent not being strong enough not to screw
myself.

last New Year's Eve it all rose to the surface
and grabbed my mind and I

threw the tree to the floor, lights, decorations
and all.

a foul business.
the next day I felt obligated to clean things up
myself
and cut my fingers on shards of broken
ornaments.
God's punishment?

well, my wife and her mother enjoy Christmas
so I'll sacrifice my god-damned soul one more
time.

and then there's New Year's Eve.
Happy New Year!
Happy New Year to all of you!

isn't there anybody out there who feels like
puking out their guts over this whole
matter?

or am I alone feeling that the world is running over and
through me?

what a horrible thought!

but
it's possible.

a good place

on any given day whether you are
feeling good or standard or bad
you can sit in this place
among the docks
and pick yourself out a spider
crab for $1.20 a pound
fresh and live
they will cook it for you
and you take a wooden hammer and a piece
of newspaper
to a slivered wooden table
and watch
the commercial fish boats
docked there
while you crack your spider crab
and eat it
in the sun
and suck at your beer
while the people around you are easy
and normal and tired.

yeah.
hammer that
spider crab
while
the sun shines through the
beer.

the legend

the pianist from Poland gave his first concert
in New York City.
he was not well received by the critics but
the audiences loved him.

his works sparkled with a special
energy.
he often missed notes but to the
uninitiated it
was no matter.

he played works which pleased the
masses,
melodic pieces that were easy
listening,
but still, in a limited sense,
classical.

he toured endlessly,
relentlessly,
was then embraced by Hollywood
and was soon
rich.

he had his own private
railcar.
people flocked to it, followed
it,
to see him,
to hear him
practice.

women went wild, shrieked, some
fainted at his
concerts.

he smiled and smiled and
signed autographs by the
thousands.

on one occasion
he cut locks from his
blond hair,
threw them to the
crowd.

eventually, his playing
worsened but
he went on,
unheeding.

then, like everybody else,
he finally died.

damn good show for an
average
talent.

talk about
squeezing
all the juice
out of a small
lemon.

you've seen it on the barstool next to you—

it is not honorable to sit here
staring at these walls

the horses made for a wasteful
afternoon
and I sit here
waiting.

the wine isn't
working.

but it's a bad Saturday night
for others too.

then my hand moves,
fills another glass.

this war
after all
is fought finally
to be lost.

this time
like the other times
other nights
other cities

waiting on
death.

never

squeeze out that extra poem unless it arrives by
itself.

this is that extra poem and it's not arriving by
itself

so I don't expect it to
work.

I am using this poem to fill in space as I drink
my last glass of wine
tonight.

it has been a satisfactory night: I viewed an
excellent boxing match
earlier

powdered the cats for fleas

answered two letters
wrote four poems.

some nights I write ten poems
answer six letters

drink more

but in all things
the ideal is a gentle
consistency.

now this glass of wine is almost
empty.

I watch the cars peeling off the freeway
out there.

contentment between agonies is the elixir
of existence.

the glass of wine is now empty.

good
night.

a hot sweaty day in August

we were starving
yet drinking
living in a cheap
apartment
always behind
in the rent
there wasn't
much else to
do
but screw

and I was
working away
pumping
pumping
determined to
make it

I had failed
at
everything else

I wanted badly
to make it

I groaned
pumped
flailed

5 minutes
ten minutes

so near
so near

it was
ridiculous
in a certain
sense

and finally
I felt myself
so near

and
at that exact moment
when I climaxed

for no reason at all
the alarm clock
went off

and I rolled
off of her
laughing

and she asked
angrily, "what's
the matter
with you?"

and that made
it
worse

I kept laughing
and she ran
to the bathroom
slammed the
door

and I
wiped off
on the sheet

as the clock
sat there
innocently
exactly
reading:
2:30 p.m.

news item

x-heavyweight champ
jailed for mugging a
man for $14 on
skid row.

just a short
paragraph.

I remember him.
he only held the
title for one
fight.

he just didn't create
much interest.
even
then.

comeback

coming up out of the tar and the gloom
and untold obstacles,
rising up again like some freaky
Lazarus,
you are amazed at the strength of your
luck.
somewhere, somehow you got an extra
dose of durability.
hell, accept it.
you do. you do.
you look in the bathroom
mirror
at an idiot's smile.
you know the luck.
some go down and never come up.
something is being kind to you.
you turn from the mirror and walk back into the
world.
you find a chair, sit down, light a cigar.
back from a thousand wars
you look out from an open door into the
night.
Sibelius plays on your radio.
nothing has been destroyed.
you blow smoke into the black night,
rub a finger behind your left
ear.
baby, right now, you've got it
all.

this flag not fondly waving

1.

as freighters large as city blocks pull slowly into
the harbor under my window
I think of all the hopeful writers who finally
were told to
sit down and forget it . . .

2.

while your woman shops for a blouse you
drink coffee in the shopping center restaurant
surrounded by clerks
on a break
complaining about their irritated lives
while you remember visiting a dying John Fante
in a small hospital room
and how his fingers on the sheet were
white like lilies
as the nurse came in
cracking a little joke.

3.

you notice the
paw prints of a cat
on the hood of your car
like a ghost walked there
only to find the cat later
curled up on the backseat
looking up at you and past
you and through you.

4.

parts of a former time, parts of a lost place,
watching an old James Cagney movie,
never having really liked Cagney
at all,
yet now
this warm impossible
sadness
as once again he struts before you
in black and white,
cocky, bluffing, obnoxious and
trivial; it's
good.

5.

in World War I newsreels
(shown many years later
in our high school civics class)
to make the Scots in their
kilts
more acceptable to Americans
the propagandists called them
"The Ladies From Hell."
but I never liked them
when I was a boy
because they had knobby knees
and I was afraid their skirts
might fly up.
also I never saw them win
anything

although I am sure
they tried.

6.

now it's computers and more computers
and soon everybody will have one,
3-year-olds will have computers
and everybody will know everything
about everybody else
long before they meet them
and so they won't want to meet them.
nobody will want to meet anybody
else ever again
and everybody will be
a recluse
like I am now.

7.

she took me to Valentino's tomb.
she wanted to steal flowers
from Valentino's tomb
but there weren't any
so she walked me around
to the other tombs.
it was shady in there
like a leopard's breath
and she found a tomb with a
fresh supply of flowers
and she quickly dropped them
into her purse

along with her pills and cigarettes
and we walked out
of the tombs
and sat down on a memorial bench
to a dead actor
who used to fuck
young boys
and we lit our cigarettes.

8.

the Gays have not only come out of the
closet, but they have managed somehow to put us into it.

9.

well, you copulate and you copulate.
you leave this one's place and you
go to that one's place
and you compare
bedspreads
bath towels
t.v. sets
toilet paper
and the contents of
refrigerators
and always it means
leaving and then
coming back again
and it means
manipulating this one
against that one.

and you copulate and you
copulate until your
ears drop off and your
teeth fall out
and you know that
never
will you ever again be jealous
of any so-called "ladies'
man"
except those who
get paid for what
you must do for nothing.

                    10.

my lawyer told me that
Abe Lincoln really did
some malicious things,
some almost illegal
and self-serving things,
and then my lawyer
went on to describe
some of them.
I was there to see him
about another
matter
and then he dropped the
Lincoln thing on me
like that.
about Lincoln, it didn't
surprise me:

history never interested
me, still
doesn't.

11.

I think of my first whore
and how good her legs
looked
as she sat
across from me
in the bedroom (that was
also my front room and
my kitchen)
and I knew then
before anything could happen
that it would never be
enough.
there were
neon lights blinking through
the window of
my 4th floor hotel
room that was
paid up one week
in advance.
I liked what I had
then.
I poured the whiskey tall
for both of us
and we drank and
waited

looking
and then looking away,
talking wordly superior
talk
(she was my
superior)
legs crossed
just so
skirt hiked
just so.

my long life has always been
only this and no
more.

mannequins

they just didn't care.
they didn't care at all.

the ladies brushing their hair
in front of my
mirror.

the ladies eating across
from me.

they didn't care.

the ladies in my bed.
the ladies shopping with me
at the
supermarket.

they just didn't
care.

those ladies in their dresses
and in their shoes and
in their
underwear.

they
just
didn't
care.

the ladies of birthdays

the Christmas ladies
the ladies of the New Year.

they didn't.

they didn't know
how

or what
for

or for
who

or for
what.

they just didn't
know.

they watched t.v.
they walked the sidewalk.
they washed the dishes.
they put flowers in vases.
they sat by the window.

and never
never
ever
knew
or
cared.

my answer

"why does he have to use words like *that*
in his writing?"

"words like what, mother?"

"well, like 'motherfucker.' "

"some people talk like that, mother."

"people he knows?"

"yes."

"but why does he *associate* with
people like *that*?"

because, mother-in-law, if I only associated with
people like you
there'd be nothing to write about that
the motherfuckers would care to
read.

under the suckerfish sun

it's a horror show and it's
free, ignorance is revered
and Mr. Blankenship
takes tickets at the door.
it's crowded as they push eagerly toward
death.
lights flash, guns shoot, clowns
smile.
it's on the big screen.
the only mercy is murder.
there are no answers, only
questions.
false laughter smears the
air.
there is nothing to forget and
nothing to
remember.
the mad and the sane are
inseparable.
the dead breed more dead.
the foul sea and the foul earth
swallow all.
then the next birth
restarts the
horror.
here.

I am chastised

she was driving the car.
there was a sharp disagreement about
something.
she parked and we got out
to go into the cafe to eat
and I told her:
"without me, you are nothing.
and with me, you are even less."

she said, "you know, I really
have to laugh at you,
you are so pathetic,
when you try to act
superior!"

I didn't answer.
we entered, were taken to a
table and opened our
menus.

"I'll have a Chinese beer,"
I told the waitress,
"*now.*"

a fine madness

so many of my brain cells eaten away by
alcohol.
as I sit here drinking now,
all of my drinking companions dead,
I scratch my belly and dream of the
albatross.
I drink alone now.
I drink with myself and for myself.
I drink to my life and to my death.
my thirst is still not satisfied.
I light another cigarette, turn the
bottle slowly, admire its gorgeous
color.
a fine companion.
years have passed like this.
what else could I have done
and done so well?
I have consumed more drink than the first
one hundred men you will pass
on the street
or meet in the madhouse.
I scratch my belly and dream of the
albatross.
I have joined the great drunks of
the centuries:
Li Po, Toulouse-Lautrec, Crane, Faulkner.
I have been selected
but by whom?
I stop now, lift the bottle, swallow a
mighty mouthful.
impossible for me to think that
some have actually stopped and

become sober
citizens.
it saddens me.
they are dry, dull, safe.
I scratch my belly and dream of the
albatross.
the world is full for me and I am
satisfied.
I drink this last one for all of you
and to me.
it is very late now, a lone
dog howls in the
night
and I am as young as
the fire that still
burns
within.

a consistent sort

at the track
the other day
during
stretch run
the announcer screamed:
"HERE COMES PAIN!"

I had a bet on
Pain and
he finished
2nd,
one-half length
short.

he didn't win
that time
but he will
win soon
and you can
bet on that
again and
again and
again.

get down
heavy.

the old movie star

the one with dimples
he was handsome and dashing
he's 75 now
still has the dimples
mainly the cleft
in his
chin
and he stands the
same relaxed way,
you know:
confident and
undisturbed.

he really seems to be the
Forever Guy:
forever
the way he
was:
immaculately dressed
and speaking
only in the grandest
manner.

I was in the parking
lot at the racetrack
with Linda
the other day
we were walking in
and she said,
"I'm *sure* I saw him!"

and I asked her
who
and she told
me.

"he got onto that
private elevator that
runs up the side
of the building and
into the clubhouse!"

we looked—sure enough
the private elevator
was climbing up the
side of the building

up and up

and he was in it.

we watched.

we stared
as the elevator went
all the way up and
stopped

and he
got off.

as the elevator
slowly descended

Linda said, "Mother
loves him!"

when we saw that
he was finally gone we began
moving together toward
the entrance along with
the other common
people.

trying to dry out

I am a drunk trying to
stay off the bottle for one
night;
the t.v. has drugged me with
stale faces that say
nothing.
I am naked and alone
on the bed;
among the twisted sheets
I read a
supermarket
scandal sheet
and am dulled with the
treacherous boredom of
famous lives.
I drop the paper to the
floor
scratch my balls.
good day at the track:
made $468.
I look at the ceiling.
ceilings are friendly
like the tops of
tombs;
then I enter a stage of
half-sleep, the best kind:
totally relaxed yet
semiconscious
under the overhead
light
with my cat
asleep at my feet.

the phone rings!

I sit up in terror,
it's like an invasion
and I reach over for the
phone:

"yes?"

"what are you doing?"
she asks.

"nothing . . ."

"are you alone?" she
asks.

"with cat," I
answer.

"do you have a woman
with you?" she
asks.

"just the cat,"
I say.

"are you drinking?"
she asks.

"no . . ."

"that's good . . . ,"
she says.

we say goodbye
and I hang the phone
up
then I walk down the
stairway
into the kitchen
into the kitchen
closet
get the bottle of
1978 Mirassou
Monterey County
Gamay Beaujolais
and walk up the
stairway
again
thinking, well, maybe
tomorrow night will be
the right
night.

consummation

it's getting late.
I come down the stairway and she asks,
"did you write some good
poems?"
"yes," I answer.
I sit next to her on the couch and we
both look at the t.v.
screen.
it's David Letterman.
"all the cats are in except Beeker,"
she says.
"I'll look for him," I say.
I get up and go outside and clap my
hands and yell,
"Beeker! Beeker!
come on, Beeker!"
4 or 5 people in this working-class
neighborhood curse me from
their bedrooms.
Beeker comes walking slowly out from another
yard.
he climbs the fence with effort.
he's fat.
he drops, grunts and we walk
toward the door together,
enter.
I lock the door, turn just as Letterman
vanishes into a
commercial.

before the 7th race

have carried this notebook around
all day
at the racetrack and
have written down
nothing.

am now on the 2nd floor of
the Pavilion,
in the
men's crapper, sitting
here
within these cool
gray walls

I find solace
in a common
function:

something
at last
to put
to

paper.

morning after

I awaken
go to the bathroom
do what I do
then
come back
to the bedroom.

she's sitting up
in bed:
"you know what you
did last night?"

I climb into bed.
"no, what did I
do?"

"you pulled your
knife on the
maitre d'."

"yeah?"

"yes, we'll never
be able to go to
the Polo Lounge
again," she
says.

"is that where
we were?"

"yes, we had to
take a taxi home.
our car's still
there."

I get out of bed
walk over to a
window
stick my head
out: "holy shit,
I can't *live*
without my
car!"

"they should have
known better than
to invite you to
the wedding," she
says.

I pull my head
in from the
window
turn and look
at her: "who
got married?"

she closes her eyes
turns over
in bed
facing away

from me
and pulls the
covers up
over
her head.

heavy dogs in cement shoes

I try to keep people
out of here.
people
never
do me any good,
especially their
conversation.
after listening to them
for hours
I realize that their words have
nothing to do with
anything
that they are lonely and
cowardly
and just need to
expel their
spiritual gas
to be
sniffed by me.

no matter how hard I try to
lock them out
some
slip through
usually upon the
ground that
they have done something good
for me and should be
rewarded.

nothing good for me can be
done

unless I do it
alone.

but at times
I find myself
being kind to them
on some
foolish whim I can't explain
and then
they are there
across from me and
surrounding me.

this one night
after hours of
typing
I came downstairs and
found these faces
without
names
gathered around the
coffee table
saying many dull things.
this
particular night they
began with Celine
(they know
that I like
Celine).

"Celine went mad," one of
them says.

well, you know,
when a man goes insane
it sometimes means that
he does or says things
that seem extremely dangerous
to those who believe and act
otherwise.

I never consider a man
insane
when he disagrees or acts
contrary to
the few things I believe
have value.
I then only consider him
to be
a dull and dumb
fellow
more to be avoided
than to be
attacked.

well
this night they
went on and on
they were very liberal
and conscientious sorts
taught to
say what must be said after being
schooled in the Humanities
and I looked over
at my cat

and I
thought
my cat looks
better
knows more
and understands best;
he
doesn't have to
pretend anything
defend anything
or believe in
anything.

"Celine," I told
them, "wrote better
than any of you
talk."

"but he became
more and more
insane,"
they insisted.

"if so," I said,
"at least he first had to have
some sanity to
lose."

and that's what
they wanted:
response:
get the old

boy going
get him
pissed.

(try to talk to them
and you become one of
them.)

I
shut up and
continued drinking

from Celine it went
somewhere else.
Kerouac was mentioned,
then dropped.
and then
somebody said, *The Catcher
in the Rye*,
and then
we all knew
we all knew
something.
Ginsberg was
brought in
petted and
dismissed.
Burroughs was
still o.k.
but hardly
interesting
anymore.

Mailer, well hell,
that's big publishing, and
Olson, you know, well
those breath pauses were
out of date
but meeting him
was nice: he was just naturally
so nice
it was
frightening.
Ferlinghetti was permanently asleep
in the back room
and who could
read Tolstoy?
Poe was a bestseller
in Europe and
Hemingway would
be called a fag
nowadays and
did you know that
William
Saroyan had other men
writing
his stuff
in his last years?
Henry Miller, well, he
died.

in the morning
when I awakened

I was
sick and I
turned to look out the
window
white yellow grease of
morning
burning my
eyes.
next to me in bed
there she was.
she said to me, "you weren't
very nice
to those people
last night."

"are they gone?"

"are they *gone*? yes, you
made *sure* of that!"

"how are the cats? have we
fed the cats?"

I got out of bed and went
to the
bathroom.
there was
nobody in the
bathroom

just
myself.
it was a
most pleasant
and decent
feeling.
I did what I had to
do
and came
out.

she was
sitting up in
bed
waiting for me.
"you just drink," she
said, "you just drink and
drink. you can't face
people."

"that's true," I
said.

"my god!" she said
leaning back on her
pillow.

I climbed into bed
beside her.
and she

climbed out of
bed and
went to the
bathroom
and I lay there and
thought
the people are
gone
all the people are
gone
I can breathe and
I can stretch my
legs
and nobody is
talking
about anything.

and from my place
on the bed
I could
look out of the
window
and I could see the
tops of trees and
I could see the lovely
bridge
and it looked like
a fairly good
day
reasonable and

true enough
and I pulled the
blankets up
over myself
and
stretched out contented and free at last
until I heard the
toilet flush.

down the hatch

the god-damned ants have come marching here
and are climbing into my wine.
I drink them down.

the photos of my girlfriend's god are
everywhere:
in the bathroom
in the front room
his face fills the walls.
he never spoke about or touched money.
he died 7 or 8 years ago.
her god.
today she went to a religious retreat
to worship him.
I went to the racetrack and won
$97.

tonight she went to a concert by
Devo
some kind of rock or punk group
or new wave music.
I sit here drinking wine and ants.
and I keep thinking, shit, all the women
I meet are simply crazy
one after the other
they are simple and crazy:
legs, mouths, brains, buttocks,
ears, feet
all wasted
on them.

even the ants know more.
I drink them and with
them.

this is what is called a
confessional poem.

tragedy?

the cat sprayed on my
computer
and knocked it
out.

now I'm back to the
old
typer.

it's
tougher.
it can handle
cat spray, spilled beer
and wine,
cigarette and
cigar ashes,
damned near
everything.

reminds me of
myself.

welcome back,
old boy,
from the
old boy.

listening to the radio at 1:35 a.m.

I switch the station:
a man plays the piano in grand
fashion.

somewhere else
there are nice homes
on the ocean shore
where you can
take your drink
out on the veranda
and
stand at ease and
watch the waves
listen to the waves
crashing in the dark
and yet
at the same time
you can feel crappy there
too—

just like me now
having a dog fight
fighting for my life
within these 4 walls
20 miles inland.

perfect silence

all those smoldering
eyes
all that sweet
understanding
all that
mascara
all those
earrings

all those warm
bodies

will now go
elsewhere.

I realize
that
I might be
missing
my
final
chance

by leaving
the phone
off the
hook.

now
I only
phone out
for an

ambulance,
firemen or
the police.

I'm back to
where I was
years ago:
I don't want to
hear the good news
of the human
voice.

I keep it
off the
hook.

I am now
not
for whom the
bell
tolls

let it toll
for
you.

mirror mirror on the wall

your imagination, she said,
is out of control,
you overreact, your temper is
uncertain and you're
screwing me too much.

I watch her in front of the mirror
combing her hair
angrily.

I grab her from behind
turn her
and kiss her.

she drops her comb
and kisses back.

instead of going to the store
she leads me to her
bedroom.

well, you know, it was very good
all over
again.

parts dept.

listen, she said,
I never knew my husband had such a big cock.
he was the only man I'd ever been to bed
with
then I met you.

listen, I told her, do you hear me talking about
my x-wife's genital organs?

you don't ever talk about your x-wife,
she said.

well, until I met you I thought *she* had a big
one, I said.

big what? she asked.

automobile, I said, now let's put on some records
and dance.

dear editor:

remember when you
bought me that
big rebuilt standard
typewriter
when I was living on air
and beer
over at that place
on DeLongpre?

and I tried it
out
and phoned you that
night
drunk
complaining that it
jumped an extra space
when I hit an "e" or
a "u"?

well, I've just
ordered a $700
IBM electric
with my gold
American Express
card.

it has an automatic
error-eraser
among its many other
features.

I'm going to hell
so fast
you'd never believe
it.

I might have to
forget expensive German wine
and go back to beer
in order to find
myself
again.

meanwhile, I
await
delivery.

lack of a common interest

the 3 sisters were always arguing
with each other and the object and subject of
their arguing was always the
same: MEN.

they loved to party and dance and
flirt, and one of them was always getting
married or another divorced
and the babies piled
up.

but meanwhile
they were always most excited about
the next
MAN.

I sat with the 3 of them
on many a long morning
as they chatted over their coffees about
MEN.

"pardon me, girls, but I've got to
go . . ."

"where are you going?"
the one I was living with would
ask. "going to look for
trouble?"

"now, honey," I'd say, "don't talk
like that, your mother sure wouldn't like
to hear that kind of talk . . ."

and I'd drive down to the nearest bar
where nobody talked at all, I'd
get my drink and sit there
and that warm bar looked real,
friendly and good, and that
little beer sign up there with the
bubbles running through the red and
yellow and blue neon tubes, that
looked good too and they
were all that I wanted or
needed
then.

I'm upstairs now

I have given up
most of my
life
to salvage
your
life
and what
do
you do?

but

puke on my
efforts
in the
dwindling
moonlight

as

old
Bobby Dylan
tapes
rumble
like
thunder
up from

your
Dante's
playground
below.

as Buddha smiles

the ladies in blue and green and red,
the ladies in all their colors,
circle about.

                *

there is nothing quite like
the arrogance of a
beginning writer
unless it is the conceit
of
a successful
one.

                *

anger
is but a mask
that covers
nothing.

                *

looking at her
sitting at the bar

she's the best thing
in sight:

silent, blazing,
nowhere.

                *

the same sun
mixed and grinding

dancing toward what's left of your
mind.

*

I keep pondering the
imponderable.
Adam and Eve without belly buttons?
and if so, why?

*

at times
small children
wake up screaming
as something
leaps toward them
that they have never
seen
before.

*

if we can laugh, fine.
and if we've got to cry, we've
got to cry.

*

summer followed summer
flea fucked flea
as my parents
prepared themselves for an
early grave.

*

the 3 a.m.
radio sings
as a
squadron
of diminutive
flying bugs now
rush in to
keep me
company.

*

as the swans circle
the truly damned are the
truly talented
as the swans circle
the truly talented are the
truly damned
as the swans circle.

*

it's easier
to write a symphony
than it is to love
and respect
your neighbor

*

head down
sitting by the
fireplace
staring at my

shoes
as the wife tells me
how well I'm
doing.

*

anybody can be a genius
at 25. at 50, it takes
some
doing.

*

I think of Li Po
so
many centuries ago
drinking his wine
writing his poems
then
setting them
on fire
and sailing them
down the river
as the emperor
wept.

*

I light another cigarette
and wait patiently for lady
luck to
arrive.

*

we've just got to get rid of
all those poor souls
who eat pizza and go to
baseball games.

*

I shot the cat
stole a Webster's dictionary
and ate a green apple.

*

the same sun
mixed and grinding
dancing toward what's left of your
mind.

*

O my God
all that blue sky
senseless

*

I take my prickly heart and
throw it away
as far into the dark as possible and
laugh.

*

I am
like a bug
a dog
a flower.

the knife cuts into the
sun.
the plate
breaks.
the cat yawns.

     *

the once young
hero has grown
old
as Buddha
smiles.

what have I seen?

I like your way, Catullus, talking plainly about the
whore who claims you owe her money, or about
that guy who smiled too much—who cleaned
his teeth with horse piss, or about how the young poets
come with their blameless tame verse, or about
how this or that guy married a slut.

you come right out and say things cleanly,
you're not like the others; but, listen, Catullus,
didn't I see you at the racetrack bar last
Thursday? you had this great whale of a cunt
with you, she must have scaled 190, one breast flopped
loose, in a lavender dress, I believe I heard
her pass wind,—her teeth green, her buttocks
of sagging celluloid, and you drunk and pawing
her . . .
surely, that was not you, Catullus, at the racetrack
bar last Thursday?

a correspondent wrote bitterly:

"in your last book
you had 43 poems
which either talked about
death directly
or referred to it
in an
oblique
manner . . ."

I folded his letter
neatly
and placed it on the
pile
with the
others

and like the
dead
I
didn't
reply.

moving toward age 73:

yes, it's true—I'm mellowing.
in the old days
to cross my room you'd have to
step around and between empty
bottles.
now after I empty them
I stack them neatly in paper
cartons.
I'm a good citizen now, I save
the bottles for the city of Los
Angeles to
recycle.
and I haven't seen the inside
of a drunk tank for a good ten
years.
(I lock the door when I drink
and only inflict damage upon
myself.)
boring, isn't it?
but not too bad, listening to
Mahler as the walls
dance.
as a recluse it's enough for
me.
so now I'm turning the streets back
over to you,
tough guy.

I saw a tramp last night

the way the old dog walked
with dotted, tired fur
down nobody's alley
being nobody's dog . . .
past the empty vodka bottles
past the peanut butter jars,
with wires full of electricity
and the birds asleep somewhere,
down the alley he went—
nobody's dog
moving through it all,
brave as any army.

mountain of horror

in class
in high school
we were seated
alphabetically
so Burns was always seated
directly behind me.
he was the largest lad in the
class of '38.
he was tall and wide
but all of it was strangely
soft.
he was simply a gross
human
being,
and if you showed him any
sympathy or
kindness
he edged right into
your territory and
drowned you with
slobbering
gratitude.

he was at my back
at my neck
in the seat behind
me
in biology
in civics
in English,
I could hear him

breathing,
wheezing,
it never stopped,
I was conscious of
each inhale and
exhale.
I could even hear
him
shifting his great weight
about.

I mean, he tasted
like hell in my
mouth and brain
an hour here,
an hour there,
and then another
hour in
some other
class.

and worst of
all, the poor dumb
cluck
thought he was
clever.

one of his
games was to tap
me on the back
and whisper,

"it's from
Mary Lou . . .
she said to give
it to you . . ."

and he'd hand me
the little folded
note:
"big boy, I want
to be with you
so bad!
I can't take my
eyes off you!"

I'd ignore
him.

then he'd poke me
in the back,
hissing and
wheezing,
"hey, hey, she wants
you!
you gonna pass
on ass?"

I wouldn't
answer.

a few moments
would go by and

116

then he'd dig his
finger into my
back
again.

"hey, hey, you gonna
pass on ass?"

oh yes, he was a funny
guy.

throughout the class
I'd have to listen to many
other remarks:

"hey, Hank, let's you
and I be buddies,
pals.
I got a beer
connection, we can
get stinko
together."

"hey, Hank, what did
the snow-blind
Eskimo say to the
female
walrus?"

"hey, Hank . . ."

on top of that he
had body
odor.
he always wore the
same dirty green
wool sweater
even on the hottest
days.

and after each
class
he'd attempt
to exit with
me, and
follow me down
the hall.

"hey, Hank, wait a
minute . . ."

he was slow, he had
huge feet in enormous
square-toed black
shoes
and he often
stumbled
as he
walked.

"hey, Hank . . ."

I knew that he was
lonely but I couldn't
embrace his
loneliness.
he made me feel
physically and
mentally
ill.
besides that,
my life in addition to
Burns
was wretched
enough.

I had him on my
neck for two
years.

then one day he
poked me in the
back,
"hey, this one's
from Caroline!"

I opened the note
and it read,
"Henry, you are the
yummy yummy man
of my dreams . . ."

I turned in my seat
and looked at
him.
he wore large
round glasses
with thick black
rims.
his red
wet lips were
twisted into an
asinine
grin
and I said,
"listen, Burns, if
you ever touch me
or ever speak to
me or even look
at me again, I promise
you, I'm going to
kill you."

then I looked
away.

Mrs. Anderson, the
English teacher
said from her
desk, for all to
hear:
"Mr. Chinaski,
I'll see you

after
class!"

and I did.
I stood there
as she looked up
at me from her
desk.

"I've noticed
your horseplay
all term long.
what do you
have to say about
it?"

I didn't
answer.

"Mr. Chinaski, I
am going to give you
an 'F' in English."

"all right . . ."

"you can go
now."

I didn't attend that English
class
after that

but I still saw Burns
in a couple of
other classes.

and thankfully I didn't have to
kill him.

all I heard was his
breathing,
his wheezing.

and worse, I began
to feel guilty
as if I had perpetrated
some hideous unkind
curse on
him.

I felt as if I had locked
him away
in some terrible
prison,
in some dank and
lonely
place.

but I left him
there.

sitting
at the back of
my neck

class of Winter
'38.

the last winter

I see this final storm as nothing serious in the eyes of
the world,
there are more important things to worry about and to
consider.

I see this final storm as nothing special in the eyes of
the world
and it isn't special.
other storms have been greater, more dramatic.
I see this final storm approaching and
my mind waits.

I see this final storm as nothing serious in the eyes of
the world.
the world and I seldom agree on most
matters.
but now we can agree.
bring it on, bring it on.
I have waited too long now.

bent

near the belly of the sun,
undone by lambs,
the red bottle's babble,
tight shoes,
right turns,
the gibbering ladies,
the macho men,
rusty bells,
all the alarms,
all the hospitals,
the jails,
I've gone mad here,
now,
measuring the death of
time.

as white light runs past
like a dog,
where did it go?
where did it all go?

bayonets in candlelight

as the birds spit curses at you and
while the prisons empty their half-dead
into your silken lap,
I see the fine whiskers of a rat
exploring my bottled and discouraged floor:
fat, fat, this crawling angel
and there is a book by Rimbaud and it
ignores the book by Rimbaud as
particles of the clock stick in my particle brain
like arrows working at old wounds
and christ I cannot pull them out.

you can take a butterfly and rip its wings,
you can take this room and run it through fire,
you can take my bones and paint them green
and hang them out the window like letters from Spain
but
I will be running down the hall of your granite heart
for years
and then,
with you,
not hand-in-hand but equally sorry and poor and sad,
with all the victories and defeats
safely in the past,
we'll be
like bayonets in candlelight
the voices heard, now from behind:
I see I hear I am I see I hear I am I was I was
I still am this moment
this butterfly moment staring into the round deep
eye of an empty bottle

the shade moving in the wind like a hand
once here
and now gone.

I think I think
but not too hard
and take this paper from the machine
while kicking the rat moving idly by.